Table of Contents

THE CLASSY Transgender LADY

This book is dedicated to my fur baby, Snuggles.

He passed away on August 28, 2022.

Thank you for giving me 15 years and 3 months of unconditional love.

I will always love you…

A book by Amanda Valentine

Copyright © 2022

Foreword

There are different types of attractive transgender women.

The most common one is the kind who puts
everything out in the open.

She's the stereotypical attractive woman who knows
that she has it and flaunts it every chance she gets.

You'll probably see her poorly dressed on most occasions.

The kind that dresses up provocatively even if she's just
buying carrots and fresh milk from the grocery store.

While she's successful in grabbing people's attention,
her presence becomes prematurely forgettable.

This is because her beauty is overshadowed by her desperation.

Now, there's the kind of transgender woman
who's more subtle about her powers.

She knows when, where, and how to wield them.

Even if she's dressed up casually, her
elegance emanates effortlessly.

The power that she holds goes beyond grabbing attention.

Her presence is like an apparition and people will always
remember the memory that her cameo leaves.

She is The Classy Transgender Lady.

In this book, I'm going to teach you everything about her.

You have everything that it takes. You just
need to read the manual.

Tip 1 – Timelessness isn't Trivial

Every classy transgender lady knows that when it comes to style, classics trump everything else.

They do not invest in anything that comes and goes. Money doesn't grow on trees and they're not going to impulsively buy a crop-top shirt just because everyone on social media is wearing it.

Whenever you buy something, whether it be a piece of clothing or an accessory, you have to think about whether you can wear it again after 10 years.

If you don't, it's probably not worth your money.

Now, if all else fails, ask yourself, "What would Audrey Hepburn do?".

Can you picture her wearing an oversized tee paired with hot pants and uggs?

No, you can't. Because frankly, Audrey wouldn't be caught dead in such an ensemble.

Added to that, you must also avoid graphic tops. Only wear them in support of a movement and only on occasions.

Affirmations are really helpful but wearing a t-shirt that says "Boss Babe" doesn't make you a boss babe, it makes you look juvenile.

Besides, real boss babes wouldn't do such a thing. They won't prove anything by wearing a $5 uninventive piece of clothing.

Tip 2 – Classy Colors

Believe it or not, classy colors exist.

They mostly come in neutral and pastel tones.

While bold colors such as red and hot pink can also look classy, those should only be utilized by experts.

As a novice, I highly recommend you to stick to:

- White
- Beige
- Tan
- Black
- Pastel Pink
- Pastel Blue

Also learning about the basics of Color Theory will greatly help you to figure out what shades best suit your skin tone.

Wearing colors that don't go well with your skin tone will wash your face out.

Instead of wearing the clothes, they will wear you.

There are 3 common types of skin tones–warm, neutral, and cool.

Anything that has tints of yellow and red will look good with warm skin tones.

Cool tones can capitalize on greys, blues, and blacks.

The ones with neutral tones can wear anything flawlessly so if you happen to belong to this group, congratulations!

Tip 3 – Hair Care

A classy transgender lady will never be caught dead looking like a damp poodle.

Most people put so much importance on makeup that they tend to forget that the magic happens with the hair.

Subtle hair flips and bounces when then correctly can leave lasting memories.

People will easily forget your makeup look but will always remember what your hair looks like.

Take it from profilers. When there's a criminal investigation, the type of makeup isn't part of the question. Officers often ask about the height, weight, skin color, and ding ding ding… hair!

Bun Bonanza

Many classy transgender ladies know how to create a daily effortless bun.

A bun automatically elevates one's look and helps put emphasis on a person's facial features.

Also, it makes one look like a graceful ballerina and that's the type of elegant touch that nobody can ignore.

Healthy Hair

Classy hair comes in all textures but the nuance that often makes hair look classy is if it's healthy.

Regular trips to the salon and a religious home hair care routine will help you achieve it.

Healthy hair often looks shiny and doesn't have split ends.

Avoid too many Accessories

Moreover, it's vital not to put too many hair accessories. Doing this will downgrade your look and can give an impression that you're an extra for a musical.

Hair Length

Hair that's too long also kills elegance.

While long luscious locks are attention-grabbing, the wearer can look comical and like she's trying too hard.

It can also give an impression of being unkempt.

Most importantly, it also gets everywhere!

It may dip on your food, the passenger behind you on the same flight, and the person receiving the blow from your hair that's being carried by the wind on a bus stop.

Something before the bra line will make you look classier and will tell the world that you frequent the salon and take good care of your looks.

Layered Locks

Fringes and layers will help frame your face and highlight your face's best features.

Determine your face shape or go to the salon and find the best hairstylist.

While a lot of men like straight long hair, not everyone looks good in it.

Ornery Ombre

Don't ever do this to yourself if you want to look classy. Highlights and lowlights are fine but mismatched colors of your hair roots and the rest of your hair will make you look dirty.

Rarely will you see a classy transgender lady with neglected hair roots.

Tip 4 – Skincare and Makeup

Before being a makeup expert, you must be a skincare expert first.

A lot of classy transgender ladies don't put on too much makeup.

Part of their *je ne sais quoi* is how effortlessly immaculate they look.

While they do a lot of things to look the way they do, people will never have a feeling that they're doing too much.

That's a classy transgender lady's magic!

Skin is in

When you have good skin, you don't have to pile up too much foundation.

You're not going to look like a plastic Barbie doll. Instead, you'll look radiant, clean, and ethereal.

You don't need to spend thousands of dollars to get good skin.

But you must at least invest in the initial stages to know what to feed your skin.

Consult a highly-rated dermatologist in your area and you'll mostly find everything you need to know within just one session.

Foundation, brows, lips, and more

Now, for the makeup bit. A classy transgender lady rarely wears heavy makeup even on special occasions.

For your daily look, you must learn how to achieve the perfect eyebrows that provide harmony to your face.

Elegant ladies don't subscribe to makeup trends. They also often go for timeless styles.

Don't confuse timeless makeup with Old Hollywood Glamour.

Think more of Jackie O instead of Marilyn Monroe when you're applying your daily makeup.

Invest in the perfect shade of lipstick that's very close to your natural lip color.

If you have access to a lash perm, do it.

Avoid falsies and extensions that look like spider legs. Nothing's elegant about those.

Tip 5 – Table Manners

If you want to be a classy transgender lady, you have to possess good table manners.

It's also important to know what utensils to use in seven-course meals but we'll tackle that in the future.

Let's settle for something more actionable for today and that's the fundamentals.

Chew your food properly

Our parents have taught us early on not to open our mouths while we chew our food.

It's not just because it's the right thing to do but it's also because doing so makes you more mindful of the people around you.

Don't put others off from their food because their view is the crushed spinach and beef combo on your mouth.

Nobody's taking away your food from you

Added to that, don't eat your food like you're being hustled.

Did you know that it takes an hour on average for a Parisian woman to finish her food?

Not only will it prevent you from making a mess of your clothes. It will also help you digest your food better.

Sounds

Have you ever eaten with someone who eats their food like they're participating in a sword fight?

If so, you probably know how irritating it is.

Don't be this type of person. Make minimal sounds when you eat your food.

The key to doing so is again, not to eat like you're being hustled.

The Stem is not Ornamental

If you're eating out and the glass has a stem, use it.

Whether you're drinking wine, water, or champagne, it's always a must to use the stem.

No, you will not look like you're trying too hard. Only people without an elegant bone in their body will resent you for having proper etiquette.

Besides, glasses with stems are often clear. If you don't hold them by the stem, you're going to turn your glass into something like a piece of evidence from a crime scene–too many fingerprints!

Moreover, when you have lipstick on, always drink on the same rim where you left a pigment. You don't want to create a dirty border of lipstick swatches your glass.

Tip 6 – Your Reputation

A classy transgender lady has a spotless reputation.

Avoid scandals, fights, and vulgarity whether it be online or offline.

Don't be a Keyboard Warrior

If you can't be stopped, avoid posting your thoughts and the comments section altogether.

It's not that I'm encouraging you to be voiceless. There are many ways to express your opinions elegantly.

If you haven't mastered that yet, it's better to shut up than to give people the impression that you're a war freak.

You're not being paid to strip online

If you don't make money out of revealing your body, you're a whore. Not only a whore, but an attention-seeking and desperate whore.

There are many ways to let others know how sexy you are.

You have to know the fine line between sultry and trashy clothes.

Added to that, you don't have to post photos showing provocative poses.

Only perverts online will enjoy your photos bending over, sticking your tongue out, and holding your boobs together while making a seductive face.

Avoid gossip

Classy transgender ladies have so much going for them that it's impossible for them to find time to talk about other people's lives.

If one of your friends starts a conversation that goes along the lines of gossiping, find an excuse to stay away from the conversation.

Pretend like it's not a good time to talk and that you're busy doing something else.

Now, if they really insist on talking about it, don't express your opinions about the other person.

Just nod and laugh but never utter a single negative word about the gossip's target.

These words may be used against you in the future!

Tip 7 – Demeanor

You will fail to be a classy transgender lady if you don't have a classy demeanor.

Being classy is not a dress-up game. It's a lifestyle.

Winning Walk

The way you walk and act are the foundations of your elegance.

Sway your hips subtly when you walk. It will make you look more feminine and elegant. Don't overdo it, you're not participating in a swimsuit competition.

Gestures

Moreover, when you gesture to something, don't act like you're doing *The Robot*. Always make graceful movements. What this means is that you should execute everything like you're a ballerina. Don't mistake it with being glacial, Miranda Priestly will not appreciate that.

Talking Tricks

A classy transgender lady's mouth is never vulgar and loud.

Even when provoked, she will never exhibit this behavior.

Added to that, also be mindful most especially if you're feeling a lot of emotions.

Sure, it's such a happy moment when you reunite with your friends. But you guys don't have to scream like hyenas in a restaurant lobby like an accident just happened.

She loves everyone, even her enemies

If you want to be classy, don't wear your emotions on your sleeves.

Don't exhibit rude behavior to workers. They work for the company and they're not your slaves.

Added to that, don't engage with your haters and bashers. No reaction, no final statements... nada!

Give them absolutely nothing and kill them with kindness. This will always work in your favor.

Respect and Modesty

A classy transgender will always show respect even if the other person belongs to a lower social status.

Part of her charm is her humility. Elegance ends at the very moment that you discriminate against people who don't belong in your circle.

You must always humble yourself and respect people from all walks of life.

Tip 8 – Drawing Boundaries

Every elegant lady knows how to draw boundaries.

Never let anyone abuse and use you. You're too special to take on such a pathetic role.

Whether it be friends, family, or partners, don't let other people treat you like a doormat.

Moreover, don't be *The Class Clown*.

Being humble and self-deprecating are two different things. If you always make fun of yourself and expressly look down on yourself to others, they will lose their respect.

As a transgender woman, you should know the power of transformation firsthand.

Erase the stereotypes that people have associated with us for many years.

Don't be another CNN documentary.

Live a life of Love, Luxury, and Legacy.

You're going lots of places my dear Classy Transgender Lady.

Dating Rich Men for Transgender Women

Get Your Copy

Dating Rich Men for Transgender Women is a step-by-step guide to attracting an affluent male partner. It is a proven formula that Amanda Valentine has used for many years of reading psychology books and dating rich men.

Most people tend to think that dating transgender women is the last resort for men. On the contrary, a lot of powerful males are attracted to transgender women.

Amanda has dated C-Suite Executives and other High-ranking Professionals in Global Corporations.

She created this guide to share her learnings of what rich men truly want in a transgender woman.

Discover your inner maneater and wield your feminine power to get the man you truly deserve.

Beauty Secrets of Transgender Bombshells

Get Your Copy

We all have a bombshell within us. Some just don't know how to unleash it yet.

Transgender women are like witches. We have the power to put men under our spell if we choose to do so.

If you haven't discovered your feminine power yet, I'm here to help you.

With many years of physically transitioning, I've learned many beauty secrets from transgender bombshells.

Their impeccable beauty maintenance routines, eye for style, and natural knowledge of seduction are all going to be revealed in this intimate tgirl-to-tgirl talk.

Dating Transgender Women for Gentlemen

Get Your Copy

Dating Transgender Women for Gentlemen is a collection of trans women's real experiences in the ever-punishing world we all call online dating.

Let Amanda Valentine's 13 years of bad romance tell you what trans women truly want in a life partner.

Author's Message

Dear Ladies,

Thank you very much for purchasing and reading The Classy Transgender Lady.

For a writer, I can't seem to find the best word to describe how grateful I am for your support.

If you enjoyed this book, kindly give it a rating on Kindle.

Let's get it to the overall bestseller list <3

Should you feel the need to send me a message concerning this book, your love life, or just about anything, please feel free to follow the pages below and subscribe to my mailing list to get updates on new releases.

Homepage (www.dtwfgbook.com)

Facebook (DTWFG Community)

Twitter (Personal Account)

My Transgender Date Column (My Latest Articles)

Cover Design by Freepik